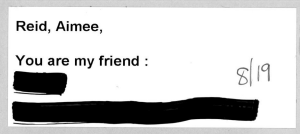

Reid, Aimee,

You are my friend :

8/19

P9-DEP-266

You Are My Friend

The Story of **Mister Rogers** and His **Neighborhood**

Words by
Aimee Reid

Pictures by
Matt Phelan

Abrams Books for Young Readers • New York

In the springtime, when everything was growing and green,

Freddie Rogers had to stay inside.

Flowers made him sniffle.

Plants made him sneeze.

Freddie had allergies.

Freddie had other illnesses, too.

He spent many days in bed.

Sometimes he had to stay inside for weeks at a time.

Being sick made it hard to make friends.

Often, when Freddie felt sad or mad, lonely or scared,

he kept his feelings inside, but he wanted someone to know how he felt.

Freddie found that he could talk about his feelings with puppets.

He gathered them around him on his bed.

That way it seemed as though he was with a whole group of friends.

When Freddie went to school, sometimes he was bullied. Neighborhood boys yelled mean words at him as they chased him down the street.

Grown-ups told Freddie to pretend the mean words
didn't hurt, but they did.
Hiding his feelings didn't work.
They just grew stronger.

Sometimes, when he was all alone, Freddie cried.

Freddie found it difficult to speak out about his feelings,
but he learned he could express them on the piano.

If he was angry, he played loud,
low notes that sounded like thunder.

He played high, sweet notes for happiness.
Freddie felt better after he shared his feelings through his music.

Freddie's mother gave him a way to deal with his worried feelings.
She told him to look for people who were helping.

Freddie began to look for helpers right in his own neighborhood.
He liked to visit Mama Bell Frampton.
She welcomed him and showed him how to
make toast sticks all by himself.
Freddie liked the good feeling of learning
something new from his neighbor.

Fred's Grandfather McFeely was an important friend.

Fred loved to visit his grandparents' farm with its big stone wall.

One day, Fred went into the room where all the adults were talking.

No one looked his way.

Fred asked if he could walk on the big stone wall.

Then everyone looked his way!

Most of the grown-ups said, "No! You might get hurt."

But Grandpa McFeely said, "Yes."

Fred climbed

and walked

and then even ran on the wall!

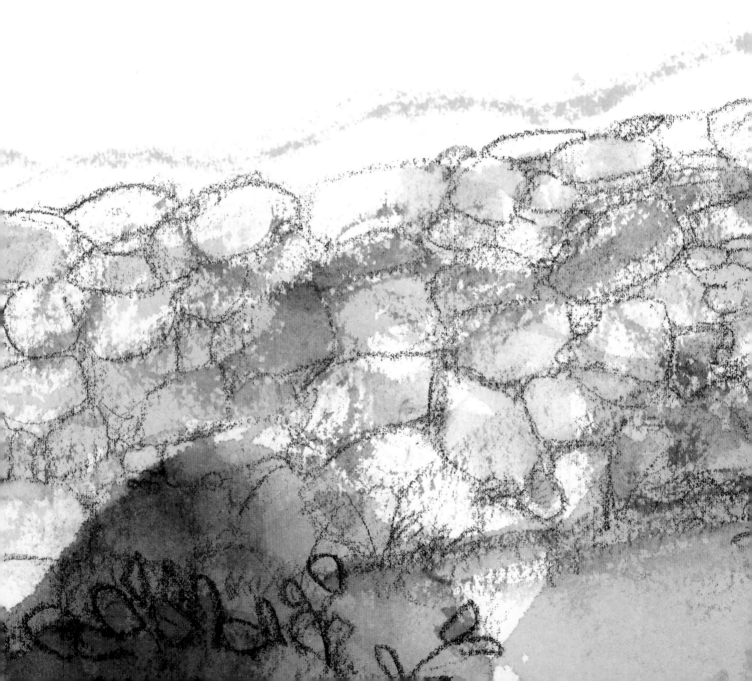

When at last Fred came back inside,

he had a skinned knee, but he was happy.

His grandpa told Fred that he liked him

just the way he was.

He said Fred was special and that,

just by being himself,

Fred made the day special, too.

Fred let those words sink deep inside him.

As he thought about them, he felt braver.

He began to speak up.

He tried new things.

He reached out and made friends—
even with people who weren't like him.

One day, when Fred
was grown up, he saw
a television program.
People were throwing
pies in each other's faces.
Fred did not like the
pie throwing, but he
thought television
could be wonderful.
What if, instead of
showing people fighting,
TV could show people
helping one another?
Right then, Fred decided
that was what he
wanted to do.

Fred created a television show for children.

He remembered all of the people who had

helped him as he was growing up.

He thought of his neighbor, Mama Bell Frampton,

who was always glad to see him.

He wanted to share that good feeling with children everywhere.

Fred wrote a happy, welcoming song to sing

at the beginning of each show.

He called his program *Mister Rogers' Neighborhood*,

and he called the people who watched it his neighbors.

At first, Fred felt shy to be in front of the camera,
but he found out that his grandpa was right.
Just by being himself, Fred made his show special.

Fred told stories with puppets.

He played music that he wrote.

He invited helpers to show what they liked to do
or explain how things worked.

Fred took his television camera to visit a farmer who had milk cows.

He asked a friend to show how people dig with big machines.

Another helper played the cello,

and another shared how to cook.

Fred explained to his neighbors that feelings were important. You could talk about them, or you could show your feelings in other ways.

If you were mad, you could pound clay or run fast.

If you were sad, you could sing a song soft and low.

If you were happy, you could dance.

Fred helped people learn to like themselves.

He helped them to be good neighbors.

Fred never forgot how his grandpa made him feel.

Over and over, he would look right into the camera

and pass along the important words that changed his life.

"You've made this day a special day,
by just your being you.
There's no person in the whole world like you,
and I like you just the way you are."

A Brief Biography of Fred Rogers

Fred McFeely Rogers was born at his grandparents' farm on March 20, 1928. He grew up in Latrobe, Pennsylvania, near Pittsburgh. Fred obtained a BA in music composition at Rollins College in 1951. After graduation, he moved to New York City and was hired by NBC to be an assistant director and floor director.

In 1952, Fred married Joanne Byrd, a concert pianist and fellow student from Rollins.

Fred heard of a new television station opening in Pittsburgh in 1953. He and Joanne moved there, and Fred joined WQED, which would become the nation's first public television station. He and a colleague began a live program called *The Children's Corner*, in which Fred worked behind the scenes as puppeteer and musician. The puppets Daniel Striped Tiger, X the Owl, King Friday XIII, and Lady Elaine Fairchilde made their first appearances on this show. *The Children's Corner* won the Sylvania Award in 1955 for the nation's best locally produced children's show. During this time, Fred and Joanne Rogers had two sons, James and John.

In 1963, Rogers was ordained as a Presbyterian minister, with the special focus of working for families and children through mass media. He moved to Canada to develop a new show called *Misterogers*, which introduced the trolley and castle. On this show, Rogers appeared on camera for the first time.

Rogers and his family moved back to Pittsburgh. Fred rejoined WQED in 1966. His new children's program was called *Misterogers' Neighborhood* and included the Neighborhood of Make-Believe. In 1968, with a slight name change to *Mister Rogers' Neighborhood*, the program was broadcast nationally by PBS and won its first Emmy nomination. Rogers developed the scripts, wrote the music, and voiced many of the puppets.

Rogers went on to win two Peabody Awards for excellence in television as well as lifetime achievement awards from the National Academy of Television Arts and Sciences and the Television Critics Association. He was awarded a star on the Hollywood Walk of Fame, inducted into the Television Hall of Fame, and received the Presidential Medal of Freedom.

Mister Rogers' Neighborhood ceased production in 2000 after taping 895 episodes. On February 27, 2003, with his wife nearby, Fred Rogers died at home from stomach cancer.

The Smithsonian Institution's National Museum of American History holds one of Mister Rogers' iconic zippered sweaters on permanent display.

Author's Note

I didn't watch *Mr. Rogers' Neighborhood* as a child. As far as I know, my family's television set didn't receive a station that carried the program. It wasn't until I was a new mother that I discovered the Neighborhood, so my daughter Rachel and I were introduced to Mister Rogers together.

Rachel especially loved the Neighborhood of Make-Believe. Every time the trolley rolled into Mister Rogers' living room, I could feel her anticipation. What would happen in Make-Believe today? Through apparently simple songs and plotlines, the stories did much more than entertain. Lady Elaine Fairchilde showed everyone that anger could be useful. Daniel Striped Tiger revealed the surprising power of gentleness. King Friday the XIII kept us laughing at the comical proclamations produced by his need to feel in control.

As a teacher, I was impressed by how much Fred respected children. He told them the truth. He also showed them how to look for the good in the world. As a mother, I was inspired to work toward making our home a place where feelings were taken seriously and all of us knew we would be accepted for who we are.

When my third child was a new baby, I fell ill. One afternoon, while my husband cared for the children, I lay alone on the couch. Too exhausted to do much else, I turned on the TV.

Mister Rogers' face appeared. He looked directly into the camera—into my living room, it seemed—and sang a special birthday song. That very day was a significant birthday for me. Then Mr. Rogers repeated his time-honored message. I'd heard the words many times, but in those moments, I received them in a new way. I felt encouraged that, despite the inevitable challenges of parenting, I could give my children what they most needed: my unconditional care.

Stories abound of similar experiences with *Mister Rogers' Neighborhood*. Somehow, Fred was able to speak through a medium designed for the masses yet make individuals feel seen and known.

As I reflected on how to capture the essence of Mister Rogers' life story, I was consistently drawn to the words he used to close his programs. The final quotation in this book is derived from Fred's testimony to the United States Senate on behalf of public funding for television, in which he states his key philosophy. How fascinating to discover that the source of Mister Rogers' iconic message was a childhood conversation with his grandfather Fred McFeely.

I hope that Mister Rogers' affirming message reaches you and your loved ones, too. No matter our ages or histories, our hopes or sorrows, we all need to hear it.

You are important. You are valuable. You are enough—just as you are.

Illustrator's Note

I grew up near Philadelphia in the 1970s and loved watching *Mister Rogers' Neighborhood* on WHYY, our local public television station. As a quiet kid, I responded to the gentle pace of the show. My favorite part was when Mr. Rogers would feed his fish and we'd watch the fish food drift slowly down in the tank. There was no hurry. Soon the trolley would take us to Make-Believe.

As an adult I learned more about Fred Rogers and came to admire him both as a person and an artist. Every aspect of his show—the pace, the tone, the material—was thoroughly planned and deliberately produced. Fred Rogers had a vision, rooted in who he was as a human being, a vision of kindness and concern and love. My focus in illustrating Aimee's text was to help find the emotional truth of the boy who grew up to be that man. I tried to illustrate this book with simplicity, clarity, and sincerity, qualities I find in *Mister Rogers' Neighborhood*.

It was a pleasure to revisit Fred Rogers through Morgan Neville's documentary *Won't You Be My Neighbor?*, Maxwell King's biography *The Good Neighbor*, and especially by (re)watching episodes of the show I loved as a child and spending time thinking about this special person. I am honored to be a part of this book. The world needs more people like Fred Rogers.

Select Bibliography

Collins, Mark, and Margaret Mary Kimmel. *Mister Rogers' Neighborhood: Children, Television, and Fred Rogers.* Pittsburgh, Pennsylvania: University of Pittsburgh Press, 1997.

Jackson, Kathy Merlock. *Revisiting Mister Rogers' Neighborhood: Essays on Lessons About Self and Community.* Jefferson, North Carolina: McFarland, 2016.

Kimmel, Margaret Mary, and Mark Collins. *The Wonder of It All: Fred Rogers and the Story of an Icon* (ebook). Latrobe, Pennsylvania: Fred Rogers Center, 2008. See fredrogers143.wpengine.com/wp-content/uploads/2015/09/The-Wonder-of-It-All.pdf (accessed July 8, 2018).

Long, Michael G. *Peaceful Neighbor: Discovering the Countercultural Mister Rogers.* Louisville, Kentucky: Westminster John Knox Press, 2015.

Rogers, Fred, with Kathryn Brinckerhoff. "I Like You Just the Way You Are." Originally published in *Guideposts,* September 1980 (pp. 2–5). Neighborhood Archive: All Things Mister Rogers; see www.neighborhoodarchive.com /press/19800900_gdpst/index.html (accessed July 7, 2018).

Fred Rogers, interview by Karen Herman, July 22, 2000. Television Academy Foundation, "The Interviews: An Oral History of Television"; see interviews .televisionacademy.com/interviews/fred-rogers (accessed July 14, 2018).

Fred Rogers, testimony, Extension of Authorizations under the Public Broadcasting Act of 1967. Hearings, Ninety-first Congress, first session, S. 1242; April 30 and May 1, 1969. Senate Committee on Commerce, Subcommittee on Communications, Washington, D.C.

Won't You Be My Neighbor? Documentary film directed by Morgan Neville, produced by Caryn Capotosto and Nicholas Ma. New York: Focus Features, 2018.

For you, my neighbor
—A.R.

To the memory of Fred Rogers
—M.P.

The illustrations in this book were created with pencil and watercolor on paper.

Cataloging-in-Publication Data has been applied for and may be obtained from the Library of Congress.

ISBN 978-1-4197-3617-9

Text copyright © 2019 Aimee Reid
Illustrations copyright © 2019 Matt Phelan
Book design by Pamela Notarantonio

Printed and bound in U.S.A.
10 9 8 7 6 5 4 3 2 1

Abrams Books for Young Readers are available at special discounts when purchased in quantity for premiums and promotions as well as fundraising or educational use. Special editions can also be created to specification. For details, contact specialsales@abramsbooks.com or the address below.

ABRAMS The Art of Books
195 Broadway, New York, NY 10007
abramsbooks.com